Symbols of the Soul

Sacred Beasts

First published by Circle Books, 2012
Circle Books is an imprint of John Hunt Publishing Ltd., Laurel House, Station Approach,
Alresford, Hants, SO24 9JH, UK
office1@o-books.net
www.o-books.com

For distributor details and how to order please visit the 'Ordering' section on our website.

Text copyright: Susan Skinner 2010

ISBN: 978 1 84694 670 7

A CIP catalogue record for this book is available from the British Library.

Design: Lee Nash

Printed in the UK by CPI Antony Rowe
Printed in the USA by Edwards Brothers Malloy

We operate a distinctive and ethical publishing philosophy in all
areas of our business, from our global network of authors to
production and worldwide distribution.

Symbols of the Soul

Sacred Beasts

Susan Skinner

Circle Books

Winchester, UK
Washington, USA

CONTENTS

REVELATION

And before the throne there was a sea of glass like unto crystal: and in the midst of the throne, and round about the throne, were four beasts full of eyes before and behind.

And the first beast was like a lion, and the second beast like a calf, and the third beast had a face as a man, and the fourth beast was like a flying eagle.

And the four beasts had each of them six wings about him; and they were full of eyes within: and they rest not day and night, saying, Holy, holy, holy, Lord God Almighty, which was, and is, and is to come.

Revelation 4:6-8

To Tom who has a wise man inside him.

Introduction

In today's busy world we all need a small space where we can contemplate the spiritual meaning of life. In this book nine biblical Sacred Beasts are painted in their own iconic window for you to contemplate in your own way. Their symbolic significance is amplified through poems, historical sources, biblical quotations, comments, and thoughts, while short stories give a contemporary interpretation to each symbol.

If we had lived a long time ago, when life was simpler, we would have only understood our place in the universe by relating it to the natural world. Earth and sky would have embodied different aspects of divine energy and sacred animals would have played a big part in our vision. In our materialistic world we can soon lose touch with the importance of symbols that transcend consciousness and are not easily defined. Yet symbols are for all time and can be found all around us if only our eyes and ears and hearts are open. On many church spires cockerels stand, symbols of hope, the return of light and the resurrection of the spirit. Beside many gates sculpted lions sit, great guardians of human beings and their spirits.

The New Testament is full of symbolic images. When Nicodemus says: *How can a man be born when he is old? Can he enter the second time into his mother's womb and be born?* Jesus replies in symbolic words: *Verily, verily, I say unto thee, except a man be born of water and of the Spirit, he cannot enter into the kingdom of God. That which is born of flesh is flesh, and that which is born of the Spirit is spirit. Marvel not that I said unto thee, Ye must be born again. The wind bloweth where it listeth and thou hearest the sound thereof, but canst not tell whence it cometh and whither it goeth: so is every one that is born of the Spirit.'(John 3:4)*

According to Jung the words of Jesus are powerful because they express symbolic truths rooted in the very structure of the human psyche, which we also call mind, spirit or soul. Symbols, Jung suggests, transform our libido or instinctive energies and desires from a lower to a higher, numinous form. As such they underpin and respond to the world's greatest and most significant achievements, like religion and art. In other words from the standpoint of realism the symbol is not an external truth but is psychologically true and a bridge to all that is best in humanity

The Serpent or Snake

The serpent or snake represents pure energy. In the bible story of Adam and Eve it symbolizes the principle of evil inherent in all worldly things.

Curled up, papery, a snakeskin lies
skewed across a path. The snake has gone
into the grass, its primal energy
renewed, its green-gold back absorbs the sun.

A white light strikes the garden: tails fan shaped,
a hundred doves rise from the Tree of Life.
Silk red poppies open, and inspired,
the snake climbs up the Tree, from bark to leaf.

Then Satan takes its form: the Satan snake
darts to east of Eden's leafy grove
and coils about the Tree of Knowledge, sleek
and sibilant, to catch the heart of Eve.

It watches Eve and Adam fall awake
to sin and death and exile and the burden
of bearing children all of whom will make
this journey back but never quite find Eden.

THE SYMBOL OF THE SERPENT IN MYTHOLOGY AND HISTORY

The serpent or snake is a symbol of pure energy. Throughout the world it has inspired more cults than any other beast and has many rôles. Its undulating movement, the shedding of its skin, its association with the roots and branches of trees, its darting tongue, the sound of its hiss, its limb-like appearance, the way it coils itself round its prey as well as its varied habitats in wells, springs, deserts, lakes and ponds, has made it a recurring symbol in art, myth and religion. It may symbolize life, death, birth, evil, sacred knowledge and the after life.

In **Megalithic and Neolithic** imagery there are many goddesses in snake form.

In India serpents are allied to the symbolism of water and the sea.

They guard the springs of life and immortality and the hidden treasures of the spirit.

In Egypt the hieroglyph for the sound TCH is a snake that symbolizes primigenial and cosmic forces. The serpent also represents the most primitive strata of life. In the Book of the Dead (xvii) the reptiles are the first to acclaim Ra when he surfaces from the waters of Nun. When Ra was an old dribbling man the goddess Isis fashioned a snake out of his divine spittle that bit and wounded him. To overcome the pain he consented to reveal his true name.The snake is very often connected with the feminine principle.

It is thought forbears of the **Minoans** arrived in Crete sometime between 4000 and 3000 BC from the Black Sea, bringing cult tokens such as the serpent, the dove, the bull's horns and the double axe, the same symbols that have been found in Catal Huyuk in Turkey and in the Balkans.The Minoan Cretan goddess, known as Dictynna or Britomartis, the sweet virgin, carries snakes in either hand. The Minoan sun-serpent was a guardian of the household and healer of the sick. Others Mediterranean goddesses, such as Medusa, the Gorgon or the Erinnyes, are depicted with snakes in place of hair. A **Pelasgian (early Greek)** myth tells of Euronome, goddess of All Things, rising from Chaos. As she divides the sky from the waters, she begins to dance upon the tossing waves. Out of the wind generated by her dance, she creates a great serpent named Ophion who coils about her divine limbs and couples with her. Then Euronome assumes the form of a dove and lays the Universal Egg. Ophion coils round it until out tumbles all creation: sun, moon, planet, stars, earth and all living creatures.

Both the goddess and the serpent are linked with birth death and resurrection, the serpent through its ability to shed its skin, the goddess through lunar associations with rebirth.

The dogons of Africa believe the snake, with its rhythmic movements, teaches women how to give birth. The serpent serves as a metaphor for the way our lives change twist and renew themselves.

In the Near East the serpent was honored for surviving in lush valleys and deserts. On a gold amulet of Anat (13century BC) the Goddess of Ras Shamra is standing on a lion and holding a lotus of writhing snakes. The Snake goddess of Canaan is depicted in 1200BC brandishing two serpents.

In Native America the plumed serpent is its most outstanding symbol. This serpent has feathers on its head, tail and sometimes on its body. Serpents related to trees prefigure Adam and Eve: A snake coils round the staff of Asclepius, Greek god of healing. It represents the subversion of the spirit that brings about the death of the soul. It was considered the first thing that medicine should combat.

In **Ancient Greece, Central America and southern Africa** the ouroboros is a widespread symbol of the serpent swallowing its own tail. It is a symbol of eternity, the cosmic cycle of creation and destruction and then creation again. It also represents the unification of the masculine and feminine.

In the West the sinuous snake is a symbol of the wisdom of the deep sea and all its mysteries but as a desert creature associated with the 'dryness of the spirit' it is a force of destruction. In Judeo-Christian mythology the serpent caused

Eve to eat the fruit of the Tree of Knowledge and to encourage Adam to do likewise, despite their promise to God that they would never do so. Their disobedience caused them and their descendants to be banished forever from the Garden of Eden. However the snake was worshipped by the Hebrews and when, because of their disobedience, they were attacked by fiery snakes, Moses, following God's instructions, held up a serpent on a pole, so that whoever looked on it should live.

BIBLICAL QUOTATIONS

Genesis 3:14 And the Lord God said unto the serpent, because thou hast done this , thou art cursed above all cattle, and above every beast of the field; upon thy belly shalt thou go, and dust shalt thou eat all the days of thy life.

2 Corinthians 11:3 But I fear, lest by any means, as the serpent beguiled Eve through his subtlety, so your minds should be corrupted from the simplicity that is in Christ.

Revelation 12:9 And the great dragon was cast out, that old serpent, called the Devil, and Satan, which deceiveth the whole world: he was cast out into the earth, and his angels were cast out with him.

Job 26:13 By his spirit he hath garnished the heavens; his hand hath formed the crooked serpent.

Psalm 58:4 Their poison is like the poison of a serpent; they are like the deaf adder that stoppeth her ear.

Matthew 10:16 Behold, I send you forth as sheep in the midst of wolves: be ye therefore wise as serpents, and harmless as doves.

COMMENTARY

Accountability is our modern way of keeping up standards. We consume a lot of ink and paper proving that we have kept guidelines, reached targets. As if that is not enough, technology makes up for any gaps in the system. Cameras give an account of car speed, cards and codes verify our identity. We live in a world of fear where we must replace trust with technological verification. It almost seems as if transgression and temptation are words that apply more aptly to our diet than the drama of human life. And yet fundamental human nature has not changed. We still suffer guilt when we harm others and weep when we ourselves are betrayed. The story of Adam and Eve and the temptation of the serpent symbolize our alienation from innocent happiness. For we have all, in some way or another, brushed up against the seven deadly sins, pride, wrath, envy, lust, gluttony, avarice and sloth. But all is not lost for we are armed with the knowledge that God loves and forgives us, and that through him we can love and forgive ourselves and our enemies.

WHAT DOES THE SYMBOL OF THE SERPENT SAY TO US?

I open your eyes to good and evil:
I force the issue, allow you to make choices. It is I who have made you truly human.

I give you a glimpse of unity:
I am Ouroborus, the serpent who, swallowing its own tail, presents a circle of eternity. As I reveal the never ending cycle of creation and destruction I show you the unifying pattern of life and death.

I show you how to start again:
I shed my old skin and in a new skin renew my life energy,

as you may do if you shed the worn-out unproductive ways of life.

I heal the sick:
I coil round the staff of Asclepius, the Greek god of healing. Like him I am a healer, knowing the ancient remedies of the earth.

I am Kundalini: I unify your body and spirit:
By concentration and deep breathing I uncoil from the base of your pelvis to the hundred petalled lotus at the top of your head uniting your body and spirit. When you are adept at uncoiling me, I will remain in the lotus at the top of your head and you will attain bliss.

TEMPTATION

What passions we endure -desire, pride,
Fear, hatred, jealousy, the stop and start
Of love and lust. Can any words describe
The desperate strangeness of the human heart?

I know I shouldn't have seen him, but I can't resist it. 'One last time,' I say to myself. 'One last time.' It all began a few weeks ago when the tests showed I wasn't pregnant. It was as if I lost my balance and suffered from mental vertigo. There didn't seem to be any future at all for Eric and me. And then I met Jamie round at my friend Daphne's. I had seen him before, but never in the same glowing light.

Eric is pottering about in his toolshed. 'I'm just going out with Daphne,' I lie, 'for lunch and a chat.' I should have said Daphne's brother but feel appeased that only the word brother has been left out.

Eric looks up. His thick quiff of hair waves over his forehead;

his green eyes have a quizzical expression, as if he is hiding something. 'Daphne. The one you meet at yoga? You don't seem to be able to leave her alone. Has she's become your best friend or something?' He turns his back on me and bends over his workbench examining the frame he's making for the print of a little girl by Renoir that we bought together. His back looks as if it is hunched up, weeping, and I hurry away before my imagination has him pleading with me not to go. One last time, I say to myself, such is the strength of my passion.

Jamie is waiting for me by the river, or to be more accurate a bend in the river that is overhung by ancient willow trees and guarded by stinging nettles. Under the trees is a grassy patch where the world can't see us and we can forget the world. We kiss passionately then lie down side by side and look into each other's eyes. I feel sixteen again. Outside the shelter of the willows it has begun to rain. No-one will be about. With great gentleness Jamie takes off my clothes and then undresses himself. We are naked to the elements like Adam and Eve. But even the thought of that apple can't stop me and we make love urgently to the gentle swishing of the rain. Afterwards I lie in his arms until he says he must get back. They always shop on Saturdays. I cling to him for as long as I can and when he has gone I walk up and down the river bank until I am wet through. Even then I don't go home. Instead I go round to Daphne's so that my lie will turn into a half truth.

Daphne is strangely muted. She flings me a towel and gives me a pair of grey trousers and a jumper. They are too big for me but strangely comforting. Over a very hot cup of tea she tells me the shocking truth. Jamie came round a week ago and told her that I was temptation itself and unless I keep away I would ruin all their lives.

It is hard to describe my feelings. I feel betrayed, numbed, guilty and above all angry, as if Jamie is suggesting I am Eve and it is all my fault. Then I begin to weep and Daphne takes my hand.

'I'm sorry, Sylvie, ' she says. 'He's always told me things. When we were children it was him and me against Mum and Dad. They were always quarrelling and we were always crying. When they divorced we went from one to the other and hadn't got a proper home. So Jamie and me stuck together like limpets. We always have, and I suppose we always will. Don't worry, Sylvie, I won't tell anyone.'

I can't speak, I just nod. I realized how little I know about Jamie, or Daphne for that matter. Or myself. It seems as if there is only one person I know about.

I go home in Daphne's clothes, and true to form, Eric laughs at me. 'You look as if you're pregnant,' he says and puts his arms round me. 'Cheer up lass, there's nothing wrong with you or me. They said it was bad luck and all we have to do is try again.'

I look at the picture he has so carefully framed. The little girl is beckoning me back as if she is my child.

I begin to weep but Eric will never know why.

2

The Lamb

The lamb signifies purity, innocence, meekness and sacrifice.
It represents the Lamb of God.

I am the visionary lamb
Sacrificed for Everyone.
I am of ancient lineage:
In many a long forgotten age
My sacrifice was spring and key
To fresh creative energy.
From land to land my blood was spilt
To give new life where there was guilt.

They burned me on a sacred pyre:
My burning was atonement's fire.
And when the echoing years passed by
And He was born who lived to die,
Then my breath became His breath,
Then my death became His death.
Then God's Lamb hung on a Tree
To rescue our humanity.

THE SYMBOL OF THE LAMB IN MYTHOLOGY AND HISTORY

As we have already seen, the lamb signifies purity, innocence, meekness and sacrifice. But in some churches its connection with the Lion are illustrated and the significance of the Lamb and Lion are inverted. For instance in a medieval church in Armentia,

Spain, the Lamb of God (Agnus Dei)is shown in a circle that symbolizes the All with the inscription: I am the death of death. I am called a lamb, I am a strong lion. (Mors ego sum mortis. Vocor Agnus, sum Leo fortis.)

The symbol of the lamb goes back into mythology and ancient history.

Sumer Southern Mesopotamia

On a cylinder seal from Sumer (2500 BC) the divine lamb stands on an altar protected by reed bundles, thought to be the springs of creative energy of the goddess Inanna.

Ancient Greece

In the temple of Apollo Diradiotes (god of light, healing, music and prophesy) at Argos in South East Greece a lamb was sacrificed by night once a month; a woman, chosen for her chastity, had to taste the blood of the lamb so that she would be inspired by the god to make her prophesies and divinations ...

When Dionysus, (god of wine and drama) descended into Hades to bring up his mother Semele from the dead, it was the local tradition of the Argives (people from Argos) to annually summon him from the water by blowing a trumpet and throwing a lamb into the lake as an offering to the guardian of the dead.

Ancient Rome

In Rome, whenever an iron graving tool for cutting stone inscriptions was brought into the sacred grove of the Arvales, (a college of priests who were responsible for the growing of the corn,) the sacrifice of a lamb or pig had to be offered to Dea Dia, a rural goddess closely related to Ceres, goddess of the corn.

Africa

The Madi or Moru tribe of Central Africa, whose chief wealth is their cattle, (though they also practice agriculture) kill a lamb sacramentally. on certain solemn occasions. People of all ages assemble round a circle of stones by the side of a narrow path. A boy leads a chosen lamb round the circle four times and the people pluck bits of fleece and place them in their hair and on their body. The lamb is led up to the stones and killed by a priestly man who takes some of the blood and sprinkles it four times over the people. He asks the people to show kindness to each other, and every one, having placed a leaf in the circle of stones, goes joyfully away.

BIBLICAL QUOTATIONS

Isaiah 11:6 The wolf also shall dwell with the lamb and the leopard shall lie down with the kid; and the calf and the young lion and the fatling together; and a little child shall lead them.

Revelation 19:7 and 9 Let us be glad and rejoice , and give honour to him; for the marriage of the Lamb is come , and his wife hath made herself ready ... Blessed are they which are called unto the marriage supper of the Lamb.

John 1:29 ... Behold the Lamb of God which taketh away the sin of the world.

John 1:36 And looking upon Jesus as he walked, he saith, Behold, the Lamb of God!

COMMENTARY

Sacrifice is not a word we often hear publicly and when we do we tend to think of great sacrifices, such as the one Jesus made.

We do not, however, always take into account the true love that is all around us and from which sacrifices flow naturally and modestly as rainfall on everyday flowers. In our own neighbourhood many people, unknown and unseen, will be making such sacrifices tonight. By meditating on them, our hope and belief in the spirit of the human race is renewed and mysteriously our own love and hope, so often dulled by the litany of wickedness in newspapers and on the television, will shine a little brighter. We may perhaps also want to meditate on the wider world and especially on people we do not know but with whom we can empathize. For instance, if we think about war, any war, or natural disaster, any natural disaster, we will find countless unrecorded sacrifices taking place, countless fragments of love that mean more than life. These small scenes are timeless.

WHAT DOES THE SYMBOL OF THE LAMB SAY TO US?

I am with you: I am protection:
I am the lamb whose blood was daubed on the lintels and doorposts of the Israelites to safeguard them when God's mighty power swept over Egypt to destroy the first born in the land.

I am with you: I am death and resurrection:
I am the Lamb of God who suffered death on a cross and on the third day rose up again that we might live in a true spirit.

I am with you: I am at the heart of darkness:
I am present at the massacre of the meek and the innocent in every age, in every land, here, now, at this moment. I listen with compassion to their cries, their confusion, their pain, their dying wishes.

I am with you: I am hope:
I know suffering and because my heart is open and loving, I know the presence of God in the dark hour.

I am with you: I am fragility and vision:
My passage through life is as frail, beautiful and meaningful as daffodils in March. They flower marvellously for only a few days, giving joy to all who see them. Yet even as they wither they store fresh life in their hidden bulbs, ready to flower again another Spring.

I am with you: I am new innocence:
Suffering in faith makes me empathic, grounded, free of deception. I acknowledge the dark side of life yet with my open heart I see clearly and innocently the divine nature of existence. Without sacrifice there is no love, without suffering, no redemption, without winter no spring.

THE UNKNOWN, THE UNSEEN

Tonight a white owl flies
Into the forest of a soldier's sleep.
Death is his dream-guest and he must keep
His youthful promises to sacrifice
His life for peace.

Tonight a mother makes
Light of her rest because her small son weeps.
She circles him, her arms are like a keep
Against the fears that batter him awake
Until daybreak.

Tonight a woman prays,
Blesses her dying lover with a kiss.

In grief she longs to give her life for his.
Across the bed the wintry sunlight plays.
'Stay,' she whispers, 'stay.'

'They're coming, Grandmother, they're coming.'

'Get away from the window!'

Grandmother stopped stirring the watery cabbage and potato soup and hurriedly drew the blinds. They stood together, she, her grandchild and her daughter, in frozen silence, listening to shouts, screams, the breaking of glass, the trampling of boots. Grandmother's heart beat fast. Last time they had taken Grandfather. This time...

She pulled her ragged shawl round her shoulders and looked into her daughter's eyes. She whispered hoarsely.

'There's no time to waste. You must go with the child now.'

'Only if you come, mother!'

She shook her head. 'I must stay and confront them. I'll tell them I live alone. There's nothing to worry about. They won't harm an old lady.'

She and her daughter exchanged long meaningful looks that neither of them would ever forget. The sound of blows, broken glass, screams, marching feet drew nearer and nearer. They hurried down to the cellar. Grandmother pushed her daughter and granddaughter through the dark hole that they had dug in the wall. There was no time to hug and kiss. The muddy passage led to the field and the river where Grandfather's boat was moored among the rushes. After the tunnel was dug out, Grandmother had crept through the passage every night to put another potato, another bottle of water in the hold. If the soldiers came her daughter and her granddaughter would escape through the tunnel and lie in the bottom of the boat until nightfall. Then they would row on until they reached her sister's house on the edge of the river. She would hide them in her attic.

Grandmother hurriedly blocked the hole with the cover they

had made out of wood and bricks. It was heavy and it was all she could do to shove it in place. She bashed it with a stick to wedge it more tightly into the wall. No-one will guess, she thought.

She hurried upstairs. Footsteps and shouts and screams surrounded the house. She looked round for any tell-tale clues that her family had lived here with her. For the first time their poverty was their protection. They had shared one spoon and one bowl, each worn one set of clothes, all slept under the same blankets. She sighed with relief. It was as if she had been there on her own.

She felt in her pocket and brought out a postcard of Moses carrying a little lamb. She thought of the Passover and wished she had some means of preventing the soldiers from coming to her door. But there was none.

She sat at the table with a half full bowl of soup, stirring it with the spoon. There was a raucous shout, a loud bang, a kicking, a splintering of wood. Three soldiers marched in. Grandmother looked up at them and smiled.

'I would have let you in. Soup?'

Her voice was calm but all the time she held the postcard of Moses and the lamb tightly in her pocket and prayed for courage.

3

The Lion

The lion is a universal symbol linked to the sun and seen as a powerful guardian of human beings and their spirits. In Medieval Christian symbolism the lion represents royal dignity, constant struggle, light from the sun and victory. Christ is known as the Lion of Judah.

I am sun beast,
Animal of gold,
My mane flares up like wings,
My tail swings.
My paws touch vibrant wires -
Messages of leaf, grass and earth.
In the birth light of the East
I am young king
But when the sun falls into western fires
I am old.

I am guardian beast,
Nile watcher,
My floods seed the desert,
Flower the inert
Dry sand. In the Underworld
I keep the dead from evil spirits, guard
The North from death. I am high priest,
Symbol of Christ, his majesty unfurled,
Wise Lion of Judah.

THE SYMBOL OF THE LION IN MYTHOLOGY AND HISTORY

In Egypt because the annual floods of the River Nile coincided with the zodiacal sign of Leo (Lion) it was believed that the lion overlooked and managed the floods. The lion was also linked with the Egyptian solar deity Ra and with Osiris who was ruler of the underworld. The lion also represented fierce and protective maternal deities and was sometimes personified as the lion-headed Egyptian goddess Sekhmet, who was the guardian against disaster and disease.

In Greek mythology the lion symbolized the power of death. When Hercules defeated the Nemean Lion he wore its skin as an emblem of victory over death.

The lion's courage also made it a guardian of the underworld. It's rôle was to protected the souls of the dead from evil spirits.

The lion is also a symbol of the sun itself and in the ancient world represents sun gods such as the Greek Apollo and the ancient Persian Mithras.

The lion is generally seen as King of the Beasts, the earthly opponent of the eagle who commands the sky.

In Africa and Asia the motif of the sun lion tearing out the throat of the moon bull is a constant theme in ornamental art.

The young lion is the rising sun and the old lion is the setting sun. Its yellow mane resembles the rays of the sun whose heat is as fierce as the lion's ferocity.

Buddhists sometimes depicted the Buddha as a lion in order to mark his enlightenment.

Hindus believe the lion is a guardian of the North, and an attribute of their goddess Durga who destroys evil.

In Christianity the link between the sun and the lion was taken up in the Middle Ages and became a Christian symbol. 'The Lion of Judah ' is a symbol of Christ and the winged lion represents Christ's majesty. It became the emblem of St Mark. The ordinary lion as earth and the winged lion as fire are both symbols of royal dignity, constant struggle, victory, light from the sun and morning. In imitation of the Resurrection, male lions are said to breathe life into still born cubs after three days.

BIBLICAL QUOTATIONS

Genesis 49:9 Judah is a lion's whelp: from the prey, my son, thou art gone up: he stooped down, he couched as a lion, and as an old lion; who shall rouse him up?

Judges 14:5 and 14:8 Then went Samson down, and his father and his mother, to Tim-nath, and came to the vineyards of Tim-nath: and behold, a young lion roared against him ... and he turned aside to see the carcass of the lion: and behold, there was a swarm of bees and honey in the carcase of the lion.

Proverbs 30:29-31 There be three things which go well, yea, four are comely in going: A lion which is strongest among beasts, and turneth not away for any; A greyhound; an he goat also; and a king against whom there is no rising up.

Revelation 5:5 And one of the elders saith unto me, Weep not: behold, the Lion of the tribe of Juda, the Root of David, hath prevailed to open the book, and to loose the seven seals thereof.

Proverbs 28:1 The wicked flee when no man pursueth: but the righteous are bold as a lion.

COMMENTARY

The power of the Lion symbol reminds us that power is a dominant theme in our lives. As children we feel the power of adults, as adults we experience the power of organizations and sometimes their abuse. When things happen to us about which we can do nothing we sense the power of fate and wonder why it brings joy to some and sorrow to others. Throughout life we are aware of the power of death. And then there is the power of good and evil. Sometimes it takes a life-shattering event for us to recognize the bad power in ourselves and to forgive the bad power in others. The Lion represents the power for good and reminds us that we too have power to receive and give goodness, though we are not always aware of it.

If you look back through the day you will find how many times good has been done to you, maybe in the form of a smile, a helping hand, an uplifting piece of music, a wave, a warm voice at the end of the telephone. Good power, whether it is widespread or local, is the essence of a good life.

We are not victims. Whatever circumstances we find ourselves in, we have the power to react in a humane and courageous way.

WHAT DOES THE SYMBOL OF THE LION SAY TO US?

I am good power:
The lion reminds us that whoever we are and wherever we are we all have the power to do good. Our arena is wide, from family, friends and neighbours to the outer world.

I am your guardian:
The lion, as the symbol of Jesus Christ, tells us we are not alone. Whatever our trouble or grief he is there to guard us and to guide us.

I am enlightenment:
The lion encourages us to meditate like the Buddha who, by understanding the nature of life and facing its sorrows, found the path of peace and joy.

I am the rising sun and the sinking sun:
The lion reminds us of the pattern of each day and of life itself and encourages us to accept it. In the morning of our lives we have greater earthly strength and are prepared to make our way as well as we can. In the evening of our lives we are less strong physically but have gained much experience and have a deeper spiritual understanding.

LION POWER

It's unexpected your direct gaze.
And though I've seen you sculpted everywhere
on church doors and cathedral walls,
it's only now your shining stare
is like a shooting star that falls
into my eyes.

It's unexpected, your secret art.
In paintings and in frescoes, many times
I've watched you, powerful, alert,
Tread unknown mountaintops and now you climb
Light as a child into my open heart,
my dazzled mind.

'Go on! In you go! I've had enough of looking after you.'

Lucy's brother Ben pushed her into the cupboard under the stairs and drew the bolt. She sat crouched up, her head on her knees, her only comfort, a soft toy called Leo. He was as small as her hand with warm brown eyes and a thick yellow mane. She held him tightly and tried to imagine that the darkness of the cupboard was really night. She and Leo were on a boat journeying to a remote island where all the plants and wild animals would play with her. The only trouble was that it was night forever.

This was not the first time her brother had locked her in the cupboard and gone off to play football. He had done it many times and he was always back in time to release her and deny everything when Mum came in. And Mum always believed him.

For three years Ben locked her in the cupboard and for three years Lucy's protests were ignored. When she was grown up she never remembered the many lovely things that happened to her as a child. It was this dark, claustrophobic experience that flooded her mind. That and the comfort Leo the Lion gave her. Even now she kept him dangling above the dashboard of her car, her guardian mascot.

And then one day her brother was driving home from work pretty fast in his old banger because that evening he was going out. He overtook the car in front on a bend in the road, certain that his car had the power and speed to deal with any oncoming vehicle. How was he to know that his sister was coming towards him in her little red car ? The sound of the crash hammered into Lucy's head. Her car spun out of hand, skidding towards the hedge. Leo swung crazily above the dashboard comforting her as he had done in the cupboard all those years ago. She disentangled herself from the claustrophobic air bag and despite the damage to the side of the car, managed to get out and use her mobile.

Her heart sank. On the other side of the road Ben's car had overturned. He was in a car that might explode at any moment and it would be several minutes before the fire engine came to haul him out. Other cars had drawn up and with her heart in her mouth Lucy crossed over the road. Ben was hanging upside down, secured only by his by his seat belt. There was no sign of an air cushion. Lucy put her hand through the broken window and reached out. Her brother was white and bleeding but still conscious. He looked at her with an expression that seemed to cut through the past, as if this terrible accident had given him some sort of inner victory. 'Thank God you are all right' he muttered. He lapsed into silence and she gently and desperately stroked his head. She could hear the fire engine clang towards them and prayed the car wouldn't break into flames.

Ben opened his eyes again. 'Sorry Lucy, sorry, truly sorry for everything. I didn't realize until now…' Once more his voice faded away and his eyes closed. As the fire engine arrived with the ambulance and police car in tow, Lucy withdrew her hand carefully from the broken window.

'Everyone's come to help you,' she said, 'It will be all right Ben. Everything will be all right.'

As she went back to her own car she felt as if a great weight had lifted from her heart. For the first time she was free of her childhood past.

4

The Eagle

In battles with serpents the eagle symbolizes the triumph of celestial, spiritual powers over the forces of evil and darkness.

I am Aquila
Bird of power.
Legions march to my call.
With open wings I shelter Pax Romana.

I am Storm Bird.
My eyes swivel, sharp and impenitent.
I bolt in plumb line flight,
Fall like a knife.

My steel claws curve, my beak,
Smooth as beaten stone,
Sinks in skin and flesh.
I hold and swing the battened snake.

I am Father Bird.
The young eat in my nest
I guard them, my wings
Stretch from night to day.

I am Spirit Bird:
I sit behind St. John
So close to his head I can hear
The tread of his visions.

THE SYMBOL OF THE EAGLE IN MYTHOLOGY AND HISTORY

Eagle myths are very old. They go back to the Hittite Empire (1900-1200 B.C.) and Byzantium and from there found their way into Christian symbolism. The eagle is luminous and shares the elements of air and fire. Because its flight is fast and daring and it is associated with thunder and fire, it is an emblem of heroic nobility, connected, like the lion, with gods of war and power. It is also identified with a male fertilizing a female and as such symbolizes the father figure.

In mythology or mythological art the eagle overcoming the bull or the lion symbolizes the triumph of the spirit over physical force. In its serpent killing the eagle symbolizes the triumph of celestial, spiritual powers over the forces of darkness and evil.

In **Ancient Greece** it symbolized divine majesty. It is connected to the thunderbolt and is depicted on Macedonian coins.

In **Ancient Rome** the eagle is Jupiter's bird. The Roman eagle or aquila, was an imperial symbol whose wide wings sheltered the Empire's Pax Romana. On Roman coins it represents the Roman Legions and also the power of the emperors.

The **Aztecs** also considered the eagle to be their imperial bird.

It was known as the storm bird, an interpretation that came from Mesopotamia and spread through out Asia Minor. In the twelfth century an eagle landing on a cactus plant was a sign of where to site their capital city, Tenochtitlan (Mexican city.)

In **China** the eagle is a fearless warrior fighting for what it right, and as such is seen as a symbol of the spirit. However, when the eagle and serpent are not in conflict they symbolize totality and cosmic unity, or the union of spirit and matter.

In **Egypt** the hieroglyph that stands for the letter **A** shows an eagle representing the origin and warmth of life, and the day.

In Vedic tradition, (the Vedas are the ancient sacred books of the Hindus) the eagle is the messenger who takes the Soma from Indra, the great god of rain and thunder. In Vedic hymns the Soma is the moon-plant whose juice confers immortality and excites even the gods. The eagle is also Garuda, who carries Vishnu, the god who personifies light. Garuda is half man, half eagle and the enemy of snake demons.

In **Sarmatian** (Eastern European) art, the eagle is the emblem of the thunderbolt and fighting.

In **Oriental** art the eagle is portrayed as Imdugud, the bird that ties the celestial and the terrestrial deer together by their tails.

In Native America, the eagle symbolizes the struggle between the celestial and spiritual principle and the lower world.

In **Ancient Syria** the eagle is depicted with human arms and symbolizes sun worship. The eagle also conducts souls to their immortality.

In Germanic mythology the eagle was a symbol of the god Woden, also known as Wodan and Odin who was associated with the underworld, magic, warfare and the heavens. In Norse mythology Odin took the shape of the eagle to retrieve the mead of divine inspiration, a treasure of the gods that had been stolen by two giants.

In **Christian** symbolism the eagle is the spirit of prophesy and a messenger from heaven. It's flight is identified as prayer rising up to our Lord, and as grace descending on humanity. The eagle then is the symbol of the Ascension and of prayer. In Romanesque art, as in Native America, the eagle is the emblem of struggle between the spiritual and the physical.

Like other animals, when it is in the zodiacal sign of Gemini (the twins) the eagle becomes two headed and is depicted in the mystically significant colours of white and red.

When the eagle is shown carrying a victim it represents the sacrifice of the lower forces and the victory of the spirit.

BIBLICAL QUOTATIONS

Job 39:27-29 Doth the eagle mount up at thy command, and make her nest on high? She dwelleth and abideth on the rock, upon the crag of the rock, and the strong place. From thence she seeketh the prey and her eyes behold afar off.

Deuteronomy 28:49 The Lord shall bring a nation against thee from far, from the end of the earth, as swift as the eagle flieth; a nation whose tongue thou shalt not understand.

Jeremiah 49:16 ...though thou shouldest make they nest as high as the eagle, I will bring thee down from thence, saith the Lord.

Proverbs 30:18-19 There be three things too wonderful for me, yea, four which I know not: the way of an eagle in the air; the way of a serpent upon a rock; the way of a ship in the midst of the sea; and the way of a man with a maid.

Deuteronomy 32:11-12 As an eagle stirreth up her nest, fluttereth over her young, spreadeth abroad her wings, taketh them, beareth them on her wings: So the Lord alone did lead him, and there was no strange god with him.

COMMENTARY

From time to time we all feel powerless: powerless before inner nightmares and terrors, powerless before death, illness and accident, powerless before guilt. Powerless before the passing of time that goes by so quickly we are left with a sense of confusion. What has happened to our other selves? What has happened to our loved ones? What has happened to our country? We are powerless before divorce and separation, powerless when friends die or become fatally ill or have a bad accident, powerless when we too are afflicted.

Our powerlessness is in the face of good things as well as bad. Why do I have food and water when innocent children on the other side of the globe are dying of starvation? Why? Why? We have only to contemplate the Eagle's spiritual power to recognize that when we feel powerless, we too have been given many gifts of the spirit: the gift of laughter; laughing at ourselves, laughing at the hopeless situation. The gift of concentration: making each moment of such importance it has its own timelessness. The gift of belief that gives meaning to life and opens up the strongholds of a heaven where we are never alone; the gift of love and friendship that have sustained many, many people in the most violent storms of life.

WHAT DOES THE SYMBOL OF THE EAGLE SAY TO US?

I carry the warmth and the light of day:
I encourage you to think of light as one of your greatest gifts. You may take it for granted, because it is constant. But it never fails to show you the beauty of your world, defining the smallest petal to the tallest mountain.

I am a fighter:
In many situations you have to be a fighter. In depression it is the fighting spirit that keeps you going, in physical illness it is the determination to overcome it that helps you to get better. In difficult situations you have to fight for the truth and not be waylaid by false propaganda or ill feeling. You must fight to keep in touch with your inner self and the Holy Spirit. Whatever the situation you must fight courageously, for courage is your right arm and your shield.

I am watchful and overcome the evil serpent:
Sometimes it is very hard to recognize and deal with evil, for what is bad to one person is good to another and at times

integrity loses out to tolerance. It is helpful to remember that when Jesus tells you to turn the other cheek he wishes you to forgive the person but not to be blind to their deed. It is the spirit that matters and the eagle represents the triumph of the spirit over the forces of darkness.

When I am not in conflict with the serpent we represent cosmic unity:
The spirit and the dark forces are within all humanity. If you can reconcile them in yourself you will be balanced and unified, you will have attained freedom of spirit.

I am the spirit of prophesy, the messenger from heaven:
When you are open-spirited you will recognize both what you should do in life and what is the right path.

ANOTHER SORT OF POWER

Had I the power I would set you free.
We would go looking for the Spirit Bird
Who glides across his mountain by the sea.
We would have no defense, no shining sword.

Our feet would touch wet grass, stone, ice-cold streams,
Sharp-pointed thistles, for earth pain is true,
Unlike this shadow play of fear and dreams
-The mind's imagining Then we'd renew

Our souls and, we would dance, but not with night
Or time or death: our spirits would be healed,
Gentle as new born feather-down, and light,
So light we'd fly above the gem-green field,

The cliff, the umber roofs, unseen, unheard
Fanned by the great wings of the Spirit Bird.

I looked round the crowded hospital waiting room but no one met my glance. Then my attention was drawn to the far wall, where three framed photographs of an eagle had been hung in a row. In each photograph the sky was deep blue. In the first photograph the eagle was standing majestically on a rock, in the second he was flying over a leaping sea, and in the third he was swooping down over ploughed fields. Somehow the presence of this great bird raised my spirits.

I had come by car but my sister was being brought from another direction and from another hospital. I knew the ambulance service did their best, but there was no knowing what time she would be here. I opened my book. It was a thriller but somehow I couldn't concentrate so I snapped it shut and smiled at the lady next to me. She was elderly and pale and looked as if she was in pain. She quickly smiled back.

'I'm waiting for the results. These days I spend my life waiting. The sword of Damocles, that's what cancer feels like.' She gazed at me in a resigned way.

'It's amazing what they can do today,' I said.

But there were some things they couldn't do. I knew that. I had been watching with open eyes for four years. Who would have thought my sister would be the victim of multiple sclerosis? She was too beautiful and talented to be so ill.

'A cup of tea would be nice,' said the lady. 'You look as if you could do with one as well.'

I nodded and said I would get it. We had begun to talk like old friends. But then we were all in it together, in the hands of other people. We had little or no power except in the way we treated each other.

We sipped teas and exchanged life stories. She had been married three times, and her men were all – Well, she didn't want to say what they were in front of a lady. But the children were wonderful. She had five children and didn't know what she would do without them. What about me?

It was my sister I wanted to talk about, not me. So I told her briefly I had no children but a good husband.

'Well I never!' She put the paper cup down on the small table in front us. It was cluttered with magazines and her cup balanced precariously.

'They're hard to come by! Gold dust if you ask me.'

I didn't tell her that it hadn't been an easy passage, that goodness wasn't enough. Or was it?

Someone called out her name and she stood up with difficulty. 'Here goes,' she said. 'Keeping afloat, that's what matters.'

At that moment there was a commotion at the entrance to the waiting room. The doors were flung open and two men came in, carrying a stretcher high up above the crowd. It was my sister. She floated above us, dark-haired, beautiful. Trapped. If only I had the power to help her. I called out her name and followed the procession through to her ward. The ambulance men eased her onto the bed and a young nurse arranged her pillows. 'I'll bring you a cup of tea,' she said, smiling.

'Everybody smiles today,' said my sister.

'It must be the weather,' I said. I bent down to kiss her. 'Is there anything else you want?'

She moved her shoulders as if in pain. 'I've learned not to ask for the moon, but an orange, that would be lovely.' She laughed. 'I've got a crush on them.'

'I'll get some in the shop.'

'Here, have these,' said the lady in the next bed. 'My nephew brought them for me but I really can't manage them.'

She was very pale but her eyes were sky blue.

'You're very kind,' I said.

As I peeled an orange for my sister I thought of all the people I knew and half knew. Their exterior was often sealed over, but inside, one way or another, most people had brave spirits.

'And it's the spirit that matters,' I thought, ' however bad things are. That's the sort of power we have all been given. It's our strength, our way through.'

My sister watched me peeling the orange. 'Just what I need,' she said, 'after a bumpy ride.'

'One day you'll fly,' I said inconsequentially, thinking of the eagles on the wall of the waiting room.

'You may well be right,' said my sister, smiling.

5

The Fish

Fish symbolize water and fertility and the continual round of birth and rebirth. They are saviours and a means of revelation.

Deep down in water silence
The fish ripples and dapples, gliding
And diving through silk-green mountains,
Pearl eyes peering below. There, long

Lost unremembered wrecks are dressed
In water weeds, undeciphered bones
Drift at the foot of the lowest wilderness,
The mouth of the underworld. The fish shines

On the sea's bed then turns tail,
Fins streaming. Now the sea breathes
Its body upward, up and up, then falls
Back as the fish leaps into wreaths

of untidy spray, into the glittering spur
of light and air and the warm
wide influence of the Golden Keeper
who nurtures new life in his morning arms.

THE SYMBOL OF THE FISH IN MYTHOLOGY AND HISTORY

In Paleolithic times fish were symbols of fertility. At Siberian Mal'ta a carved fish has a body with a pecked spiral labyrinth like a womb with a uterine passage. At Lorthet in the foothills of the

Pyrenees,a carving was found of two salmon leaping towards the genitals of a reindeer. Fish that are carved on bone are possibly phallic symbols.

In Ancient Greece this theme was repeated hundreds of years later on a Greek vase portraying a salmon leaping towards the genitals of a horse.

The Minoans saw the dolphin as an incarnation of Poseidon, god of the sea. The dolphin is also associated with Apollo, the sun god, and the water born Aphrodite, goddess of love, thus symbolizing the joining of the masculine solar world to the feminine aquatic world of the womb. This connection is underlined phonetically by the Greek word for Dolphin - delphis, and the word for womb - delphys. According to Greek mythical tradition, Apollo changed himself into a dolphin to take worshippers to his Delphic shrine. For Ancient Greeks dolphins represented love and salvation and spiritual rebirth.

In Japan there is a myth of a giant carp who rose up from its underwater sleep and tossed about so wildly it caused a great tidal wave from which the islands appeared. The carp symbolizes fertility and even today Japanese boys carry paper carps on the day of the boys' festival, hoping to influence the birth of males.

In China the fish is believed to charm away evil.

In India a fish was one of Vishnu's incarnations. Vishnu as a fish saved the lawgiver Manu from the flood and brought him the whole of sacred knowledge in the shape of the Vedas (the sacred scriptures of Hinduism). He then guided Manu in an Ark.

In Kashmir (Pakistan)it is said that Matsyendranath, otherwise known as the Fisherman, had Yoga revealed to him when he was in the shape of a fish.

Dagon, the national god of the Philistines, who lived in Philistia, an ancient country on the east coast of the Mediterranean, was depicted as half man and half fish. He was originally a fish god and later the god of corn and grain. In Hebrew Dagon means little fish.

In North Africa the great Phoenician goddess Tanit has a bird and a fish as her emblem. The dolphin is particularly sacred to her.

In North West America people looked on the salmon as a healing spirit and a sacred life giver.

In Central America the fish is a symbol of the American Indian's Maize god and as such maybe a fertility or phallic symbol.

In Ancient Egypt the Fish Goddess belonged to the nether world. The Goddess Isis was depicted as the Great Fish of the Abyss. On an Egyptian sarcophagus a soul takes the form of a fish to navigate the waters of the underworld and pilgrim sites along the Nile.

In Celtic mythology the leaping salmon was a phallic and fertility symbol, linked with spiritual wisdom. Celtic and Nordic traditions associated the salmon with human and divine transformations and the migration of the soul. The Norse god Loki fled Thor's wrath by changing into a salmon, thereby associating the fish with the concept of liberty and escape.

In Christianity the Apostles are known as fisherman and Christians who are reborn in baptism are little fish made new in the image of Christ. Christ himself is the fish who guides the Ark of the Church. For early Christians the Greek word for fish - **ICHTHUS** - was an ideogram representing the initials of the phrase **J**esu **C**hristos **T**heou **U**ios **S**oter: Jesus Christ God's Son Saviour. Ichthus is found on many early Christian seals, rings, urns and tombstones. There are also many symbolic designations of fish on early Christian funerary monuments. Fish was a food eaten by the risen Christ:

.. And they gave him a piece of a broiled fish , and of an honeycomb. And he took it and did eat before them.' Luke24:42-43. Because of this the fish, along side the bread, became a symbol of the communion, the sacrament in memory of the Last Supper.

The fish has been depicted by Christian artists in many ways: When it carries a ship upon its back it symbolizes Christ and his Church. In the Catacombs it is Christ himself. Depicted on a plate beside a basket of bread it represents the Eucharist. In the

Gospels Peter is given the title 'Fisher of men' Fishing in this sense represents preaching.

Jonah was swallowed by 'a great fish' but emerged after three days and nights. For Christians his story is a prefiguration of Christ's death and resurrection.

BIBLICAL QUOTATIONS

Genesis 1:2 And God created great whales, and every living creature that moveth, which the waters brought forth abundantly, after their kind …

Luke 5:4-6 Now when he had left speaking he said unto Simon, Launch out into the deep, and let down your nets for a draught. And Simon answering said unto him, Master we have toiled all the night and have taken nothing: nevertheless at thy word I will let down the net. And when they had this done, they enclosed a great multitude of fishes: and their net brake.

Psalm 8:4-9 What is man, that thou art mindful of him? and the son of man, that thou visitest him? For thou hast made him a little lower than the angels, and hast crowned him with glory and honour. Thou madest him to have dominion oer the works of thy hands; thou hast put all things under his feet: All sheep and oxen, yea, and he beasts of the field; the fowl of the air, and the fish of the sea, and whatsoever passeth through the paths of the seas. O Lord, our Lord, how excellent is thy name in all the earth.

Matthew 7:9-11 Or what man is there of you, whom if his son ask bread, will he give him a stone? Or if he ask a fish, will he give him a serpent? If ye then, being evil, know how to give good gifts unto your children, how much more will your Father which is in heaven give good things to them that ask him?

COMMENTARY

The symbol of the Fish reminds us of renewal and rebirth. Through winter we often talk about the spring. We walk by frozen ponds and streams, wondering when ice will free the creatures below. We cower against the North wind and look at the bare windswept branches of tossing trees. And when we see our first snowdrop, violet, primrose, aconite, star of Bethlehem or catkin, we are thrilled to find ourselves sharing in earth's renewal. Spring has come at last, not just in the world but in our own hearts!

If the earth can renew itself each year, then so can we. We have a sense of fun and lightness in the presence of puppies and lambs and all tiny new creatures, we become playful and full of wonder when we encounter new babies.

Everything in life conspires, by its contrasts, to give us a sense of renewal as the continual rhythm of opposing things give way to each other: Day to night, sun to snow, wind to calm, sleep to waking. And when death comes in all its finality we still hope, somewhere, somehow, to meet again with the people we love.

WHAT DOES THE SYMBOL OF THE FISH SAY TO US?

I am the symbol of fertility:

I am a reminder of the marvellous way in which the earth renews itself. Plants, animals, insects, fish humans all have the capacity to reproduce themselves. The energy and drive of renewal is what gives us hope.

I represent the world's balance:

I symbolize the masculine and the feminine principles that oppose each other and yet need each other. The 'masculine power of the sun is open and widespread, the feminine power of water is deep and mysterious. Yet you cannot live with one or the other alone for they are both essential to the well being of your growth.

As a carp I represent the primordial beginning of the world:
None of us can truthfully understand the depths of the
unconscious, our own primordial beginning. I remind you of
its existence and driving force, and how it is the unknown
prompter of so many of our feelings, actions and words. The
acceptance of its existence is the first step in helping us to
understand and forgive ourselves and others.

I am a healing spirit:
I am the symbol of Christ, who guides and heals all those who
wish to listen to him. His words and deeds are not for one time
or another time but for here and now. Whoever you are and
wherever you are, you can share in their power of renewal.

THE BIRTH

How did you dare,
Enclosed in a warm shell,
Slip into meteoric light?

How did you dare,
Out of the blue,
Fold air into your being,

Unseen, silent,
Its only disguise
Leaf fall, wind speak?

How did you dare
Leave your mother's clock
The homely tick-tock of her blood
For the fiery dial of the sun
And stars leaping
From the sky's tower?

I was very young and lighthearted. I jumped up on the delivery table and waited for the next crucial labour pain. All the time I longed to be close to my child's birth, wanted to physically and mentally accompany her as she made her journey into the world. Contractions came and went and pain blocked my thoughts and imagination. However, in between, I was with her, imagining her sense of loss and confusion as she left the protective calm waters of the womb and pushed her way on and up into the new element of her existence. The pains were fierce, she pushed strongly, and together, somehow or other, we made her brave, amazing journey into her new world. I was not consistent. I floundered with exhaustion and wanted to sleep in the short bouts between the contractions. But when the nurse cried out, 'Just one more push. I can see her head,' despite my weakness I pushed again so that my daughter's journey would not be too prolonged. And then, at last, she slithered out, a perfect warm red colour, her eyes tightly shut, her head covered with a feather down thatch of brown hair.

The nurse cut the cord and put her in my arms. I smiled but I was too exhausted to appreciate the moment, still unable to separate it from the long hard journey we had made together. And when they stitched me up I was in such pain I almost forgot I had a baby! It was late in the night and all I remember after that was falling into a deep sleep.

The next day things were different. I woke up, refreshed and when I peered into the little cradle at the bottom of the bed, I was so thrilled and excited I wanted this first day of my daughter's life to last forever. I remember having a bath and luxuriating in my sense of achievement. The sun was streaming in through the rather dusty windows and turned the green walls gold. It was an old hospital but it felt like heaven. After my bath I returned to the ward to peep at my daughter again. It seemed like a miracle that she had arrived in perfect order. She lay there, a little bundle of being, with eyes shut tight, as if she was sleeping away the memories of her first hideout and her long journey. She rested in perfect and unconscious trust. That is the moment when I knew I would always hold out my arms to her, ready to steady her life, come what may. It was difficult to put this feeling into words so when my husband came to the hospital, after his long journey back from a business trip, I simply smiled. He didn't know what to say either. But from the beginning he seemed to be at home with the baby. He picked her up fearlessly and rocked her up and down.

'Be careful! She's only one day old!' I said.

'I think she's been here before,' he replied with a quizzical expression in his eyes.

6

The Ass

The ass is the emblem of darkness and obstinacy except in association with Jesus, when she becomes beneficent.

The people cried Hosanna
And Hosanna clear and loud
For the Lord of all the angels
Was riding with the crowd.

He had no flag or banner,
His faith was for all men,
And he chose to ride a donkey
Into Jerusalem.

He chose an unknown donkey
And he rode him, gentle, calm,
Through the crowd who cried Hosanna,
Down the roadway, strewn with palm.

THE SYMBOL OF THE ASS IN MYTHOLOGY AND HISTORY

In India the ass is the steed of the death-gods, one of whom is Nairrita, warden of the land of the dead.

In China a white donkey sometimes represents the steed of the Immortals.

In Ancient Egypt the 'red ass' was a highly dangerous animal encountered by the soul on its journey to the Otherworld.

An Ismailian (a member of a sect of Shiite Muslims whose doctrines vary greatly from orthodox Muslims) calls the spreading of ignorance and fraud 'Dajjal's donkey' because its blinkered and literal interpretations block inner vision.

In Ancient Rome The Golden Ass by Apuleius (b.A.D.125? Roman philosopher and satirist.) presents us with Lucius, who is changed into an ass - his punishment for relapsing into sensual pleasure. Only when he has thrown off the ass and become man once again can he embrace the severe trials that will lead him along the path of salvation to the highest mysteries, the knowledge of the godhead.

In Ancient Greek myth Apollo changed King Midas' ears into ass's ears because the king enjoyed sensual pleasures rather than harmonies of the spirit.

However the ass was sacrificed to Apollo at Delphi and was sacred to Dionysos because a donkey carried the chest in which he was cradled.

In Renaissance Art the donkey often represented a range of psychological states: moral depression; stupidity; pleasure seeking; idleness; incompetence; obstinacy; foolish blind obedience.

In Christianity the Bible generally presents the she-ass in a good light. Samuel went to look for she-asses, Balaam was taught by his she-ass that an Angel of the Lord was present, Sampson slew a thousand Philistines with the hard jawbone of an ass.

At the Nativity the ox and the ass were present, and Joseph put Mary and Jesus on the back of a she-ass to escape King Herod's persecutions. On Palm Sunday Christ rode on the back of a she- ass. Here she is the symbol of learning and esoteric knowledge, a reversal of the ass as a maleficent creature. Richard of St. Victor wrote that if Christ deliberately chose to ride a she-ass it was in order to show the need for humility. 'He who practices true humility before God and within his heart, rides upon the she-ass.' Here the she-ass is the symbol of poverty, peace, patience and courage.

The wild ass symbolized the solitary desert Fathers, for the hoof of the wild ass is impervious to poison.

However the medieval Feast of Fools channelled the base instincts of fallen man in order to limit their menacing and malign effects. This 'catharsis' was symbolized by the temporary presence of an ass in the choir of a church. For like Satan and the Beast of the Apocalypse, the ass is also the symbol of human instinct, the libido and life confined to the earthly plane of the senses.

BIBLICAL QUOTATIONS

In the times of the Old Testament, the Ass was the most important beast of burden.

> **Numbers 22:25** And God's anger was kindled because he went: and the angel of the Lord stood in the way for an adversary against him. Now he was riding upon his ass, and his two servants were with him. And the ass saw the angel of the Lord standing in the way, and his sword drawn in his hand; and the ass turned aside out of the way , and went into the field: and Ba-laam smote the ass, to turn her into the way. But the angel of the Lord stood in a path of the vineyards, a wall being on this side, and a wall on that side. And when the ass saw the angel of the Lord, she thrust herself unto the wall, and crushed Ba-laam's foot against the wall: and he smote her again. And the angel of the Lord went further, and stood in a narrow place, where was no way to turn either to the right hand or to the left. And when the ass saw the angel of the Lord, she fell down under Ba-laam: and Baa-lam's anger was kindled, and he smote the ass with a staff. And the Lord opened the mouth of the ass, and she said unto Ba-laam, What have I done unto thee, that thou hast smitten me three times? (story continues in verses 29-36)

> **Proverbs 26:3** A whip for the horse, a bridle for the ass, and a rod for the fool's back.

Isaiah 1:3 The ox knoweth his owner, and the ass his master's crib: but Israel doth not know, my people doth not consider.

Matthew 21:5 Tell ye the daughter of Sion, Behold, thy King cometh unto thee, meek, and sitting upon an ass, and a colt the foal of an ass.

Luke 13:15 The Lord then answered him and said, Thou hypocrite, doth not each one of you on the Sabbath loose his ox or his ass from the stall, and lead him away to watering?

John 12:15 On the next day much people that were come to the feast, when they heard that Jesus was coming to Jerusalem, took branches of palm trees, and went forth to meet him, and cried, 'Hosanna: Blessed is the King of Israel that cometh in the name of the Lord. And Jesus, when he had found a young ass, sat thereon; as it is written, Fear not, daughter of Sion: behold, thy King cometh, sitting on an ass's colt.

COMMENTARY

We all tend to dwell on yesterday's trials or tomorrow's challenges instead of living in the present. And yet for everyone, everywhere, if our hearts are open, there will be something to celebrate today, however small: a wild flower, a sunset, a piece of music, a smile, a welcome telephone call or email, an unexpected surprise.

When Jesus rode into Jerusalem on a simple ass he honoured the humblest of creatures by sharing his celebration with her, demonstrating to us that celebration is not just for the rich and privileged but also for the poor, the ignorant, the outsider. He also shows us that there is no special time for celebration. As the crowd lined the road and waved palms Jesus knew that his death was not far away, but he put that to one side.

To celebrate is to seize the here and now and to fill it with recognition and joy, to give it special spiritual status and perhaps to share it with others. In the words of the Celtic Christians it is to open our hearts to the Heart. For to an open heart the smallest and most insignificant things will speak of God.

WHAT DOES THE SYMBOL OF THE ASS SAY TO US?

I give you celebration:
It was I who carried Jesus through the streets of Jerusalem as people lined the road, shouting for joy and waving palms.

I give you hope:
I was an outsider but one day I had the honour to witness the birth of a child who would change the world. He was in my stable, in my manger. I warmed him with my hay and my breath. You too are needed to warm the world, whoever you are, whatever your situation.

I give you strength:
I have born many difficulties in life, I have had to learn to bear the pain of evil tongues and being treated as nothing but a beast of burden. I have often felt like an alien, an outsider. Yet somehow I have not given in to these feelings. They have given me strength and independence.

I give you a sense of worth:
It was I who led the Holy Family away from Herod and into the sanctuary of Egypt. At that moment I saved the Holy Child from certain death, and Mary and Joseph from terrible grief. God chose me as he chooses you, knowing that the most humble are often the most worthy to help others.

THE OUTSIDER

Though he is a mocked creature, an outsider
With upright ears folded like newspaper
Pinned to his head and a voice that stutters,
And mostly walks on his own, like a stranger,
He has a secret, his winter fire.

And though peacocks have azure feathers
Circled in purple and gold, and kingfishers
Fly through sable shadows, swift with colour
And leopards and cheetahs move like dancers
Only he has a secret, his winter fire.

And though he is ungainly with a stubborn nature
Joseph went to his stable, seeking shelter,
And Mary put her baby in his manger
While he, no longer an outcast, muttered a prayer.
This is his memory, his winter fire.

And when, brighter than lantern light, the star
Trembled over the stable and visitors
Came, he was already at love's centre,
Drawn by the baby's gaze, the child's ever-
Lasting flame, his winter fire.

I'm in hiding. I've been coming down here for a few days now. I stay for school hours and then go home for tea. I'm an outsider.

No one comes here except me. They find it too wild. The joke is it's only two minutes from home. I go down the road, hop over the padlocked iron gate, and here I am by the river. It's wild with nettles and willow herb and purple loose strife. Oh yes, I remember what Nana told me about flowers even if I don't know anything else. And I won't ever, because I'll never go back to school again. *Never*. Not after last week. I don't care what they say.

Here are ducks and swans and the stray cat. They're my friends, especially the cat. She's black with sky blue eyes and I call her Chandra. That was Nana's name. I whistle to her and tell her stories about Nana and her rescue donkey. 'Never underestimate a lowly beast of burden,' she'd say. She died eight years ago and I still miss her. When I think of her I forget all about the gang and the teachers and welfare and Mum who doesn't understand.

You see I'm not like the others. I'm very small for my age. I used to think I'd shoot up in my teens but I'm not going to and that's it. The only kid who doesn't go on about it is Dillon, or Dill for short. He's Sri Lankan like me and we're both in the dud's class. He's really big and strong and he runs a band. He thinks I'm cute but he's the only one apart from Mum.

'It's fine to be small Serena,' says Mum. But it isn't. I'm teased rotten and last week it got a thousand times worse.

The Raiders came after me, four boys looking for an easy prey. At first they just pulled faces as I passed them. Steve Watson, who's their leader, put out his tongue. But next day he stopped me and said he was going to chop off my legs so I'd be too short to count. The others laughed and sneered. My heart beat like a bird inside me.

I sit in the long grass and tell Chandra what happened. I stroke her as I talk. Somehow it helps.

'We were at the school gates.' I whisper. 'Everyone was rushing to be on time so no-one took any notice. They threw me about as if I was a football or something. I was terrified out of my mind. I thought I was going to die. Then a miracle happened. Dill was in late as usual and saw what they were doing. He put down his guitar and lammed into Steve Watson.'

I put my head down into Chandra's black fur and start to cry. I can't help it. I don't seem to be able to make it on my own and

I'm afraid of what they might do to Dill.

Chandra purrs as I sniff and stroke her and go on with my story.

'After that Dill said he would keep an eye on me except on Thursdays when he plays football. So I went in the next day.

My heart beat fast but Dill was waiting for me by the school gates. The Raiders were there too and I would have run away if Dill hadn't held me tight and glared at the Raiders as we passed.

That day I sat in silence. I couldn't work for fear. But Dill kept his promise. He never left my side and after a while I found myself thinking about him instead of them. He was just like a big brother. So I went in the next two days just to be with him. The Raiders kept their distance but they pulled faces all the time and stuck their fingers up in the air.'

I picked up Chandra and cuddled her. 'Today's Thursday and I can't go in without Dill. No way. At breakfast Mum said 'Where's my ash tray?'

'No idea,' I said. She seemed to believe me. She's so busy getting ready for work, making up, putting on her high heels and smoking her fags she doesn't take much notice of what I say or do.

It's late afternoon. It will soon be time to go home. I watch the sun walk across the water. It makes a golden road. The seagulls swerve overhead. The water rat comes out of his hole and scuttles back. I stroke Chandra and whistle to her until I see Dill coming down the steps.

'What brilliant whistling!' he says, peering down through the willowherb and nettles and purple loosestrife.

'I thought you were playing football!'

Dill squats beside me and chews a stalk. 'To tell you the truth, Titch, I was a bit worried about you. So I told Jacko I had a headache and couldn't play. I also told him about the gang. It saves me bashing them up. He's a good Head, Titch. He said he'll make sure they'll never trouble you again. And now I know you can whistle like that I wonder if you'd like to come along - '

'Where?' I ask him.

'Where we rehearse. It's in a garage, so no-one minds.'

'But I can't - '

'Don't be an ass! You can *whistle*, Titch, that's all that matters.'

Chandra peers up at him and he strokes her black back.

'She's my pet,' I say. Then I tell him all about the wild flowers.

'Titch, you've got a brain after all,' he says.

The sun moves lower down the sky. A boat chugs along and shadows squiggle all down the river. We climb up the steps and over the iron padlocked gate. Dill smiles and as for me, I can't believe my luck. *Me, an outsider!*

Tonight I whistle in the shower. It sounds good. Maybe one day I'll become a singer as well and bring the band fame and fortune. Who knows?

7

The Dove

The dove is the symbol of simplicity, purity and, re-found happiness. In Christianity it represents the Holy Spirit.

Out of the Ark's pitched and wooden safety,
The dove tumbled into the air.
On white feathers and frail bones it flew
To find a new leaf or an open flower.

The wet sun touched its wings with gold.
The gilded dove flew into the sun.
Below the Ark rode the flood, a mere
Arrow mark on the horizon.

In its eye, its throat and will
The dove encased the song, the urgent plan
Of Noah's faith, and at the first incredible
Sight of a green tree on a green mountain

It left the sun behind, its bird heart
Quickened, it dropped down and down
The sheer fall of air and light.
Somehow the white dove did not drown.

It flew into the mountain and tore off
One green leaf from the tree, for one
Shivering leaf was enough to prove
A new earth, a new heaven.

THE SYMBOL OF THE DOVE IN MYTHOLOGY AND HISTORY

The dove, like all winged animals, symbolizes spirituality and the power of sublimation.

To the Minoans, who arrived in Crete between 4000 and 3000 B.C. the dove is a sacred symbol. A Minoan vase (1400-1200 B.C.) pictures a flying dove holding a fish in its beak. The dove represents the soul carrying the bodily fish into the underworld where it will be born again.

In Ancient Greek mythology the dove is Aphrodite's most constant attribute.

Statues of Aphrodite from Paphos, Cyprus, often show her holding a dove, while coins of Salamis in Cyprus - Aphrodite's birthplace, are stamped with a dove. In Phoenicia a flock of doves released at the festival of Amagogia, at Erys, accompanied Aphrodite back to Libya, and on return one dove with gold feathers accompanied the multitude of white doves. Maybe this was Aphrodite in her original bird form.

In Western Arcadia, in the Phigalian cave a wooden statue of Demeter, the earth goddess, held a fish in one hand and a dove in the other.

In the Christian Tradition the Holy Ghost is pictured in the shape of a dove (although the Holy Ghost is also represented by a tongue of Pentecostal fire). The Virgin Mary's attributes are the rose, the lily and the dove. The dove is a symbol of faithful marriage.

In the Judeo-Christian Tradition the Hebrew word 'Tehom' in Genesis, describes the movement of the Spirit of God on the face of the waters. The word Tehom is also used to describe birds brooding over their young.

The dove carrying the olive branch to Noah is a symbol of the end of the great Flood. In other words the dove symbolizes peace and renewal.

Similarly the Prairie Indians, regard the turtle dove, who carries a sprig of willow in its beak, as the messenger of rebirth.

From China in the Han dynasty (206 B.C. to 220 A.D.) a ritual bronze cult wagon has been found. The cart is shaped like a dove carrying a chick on its back. The wheel and the dove are solar symbols and here the dove and the chick represent the eternal return of the sun.

Some Slavs believe that, at death, the soul turns into a dove.

BIBLICAL QUOTATIONS

Genesis 8:8 Also he sent forth a dove from him, to see if the waters were abated from off the face of the ground; But the dove found no rest for the sole of her foot, and she returned unto him into the ark, for the waters were on the face of the whole earth.

Leviticus 12:6 And when the days of her purifying are fulfilled, for a son, or for a daughter, she shall bring a lamb of the first year for a burnt offering, and a young pigeon, or a turtledove, for a sin offering, unto the door of the tabernacle of the congregation, unto the priest.

Psalm 68:13 Though ye have lien among the pots, yet shall ye be as the wings of a dove covered with silver, and her feathers with yellow gold.

Psalm 74:19 O deliver not the soul of they turtledove unto the multitude of the wicked: forget not the congregation of thy poor for ever.

The Song of Solomon 1:15 Behold thou art fair, my love; behold thou art fair; thou hast doves' eyes.

Matthew 3:16 And Jesus, when he was baptized, went up straightway out of the water: and lo, the heavens were opened unto him, and he saw the Spirit of God descending like a dove, and lighting upon him.

Mark 1:10 And straightway coming up out of the water, he saw the heavens opened, and the Spirit like a dove descending upon him.

Isaiah 59:11 We roar all like bears, and mourn sore like doves.

Isaiah 60:8 Who are these that fly as a cloud, and as the doves to their windows?

COMMENT

When Noah saw the dove flying towards him with an olive leaf in his beak, he felt refreshed and renewed. We too feel refreshed and renewed when love flies towards us bringing intimations of a sunbathed land of green trees and radiant flowers. However, as complicated humans, our experience of love on earth is not simple. Love is often torn into many strands and sometimes seems barely visible. The fatigue we feel bringing up children, often disguises our love, turning it into irritability and boredom. The inability to communicate properly with our parents, partners, husbands, wives or friends, leaves us with a sense of frustration. Our love for many of our activities may lead us to a sense of failure. Why was that meal I cooked inedible? Why is my writing so pedestrian? Why haven't I got green fingers? Why are the colours I chose for my flat unsatisfactory? Why doesn't God listen when I pray? And then another time we are pleased with what we have done, whether it is cooking jacket potatoes or writing a diary, tending our plants, painting walls, or praying. Success reinforces the love that set us on these paths in the first place, and underlies our continuing efforts.

Our lives then, are full of contradictions: For while we are all rooted in earthly practicalities, our vision of love has no roots but flies like a bird in the sky. It is to this paradox that we have to accommodate ourselves. Sometimes in the middle of a busy life, a moment's quiet meditation helps us to recognize love. For in meditation we focus not on the muddle of life but on the beauty of a candle flame or a flower or someone we care about. At such moments our thoughts become untarnished and unburdened and we recognize that love is the grace and bedrock of our lives.

WHAT DOES THE SYMBOL OF THE DOVE SAY TO US?

I am a symbol of peace and renewal:
However dark the present may be I am always there to remind you that with the passing of time and the cooperation of human beings, peace will return and with it a renewal of happiness and creativity.

I am the symbol of the Holy Ghost:
I am the gift and the grace of God, the spirit within that allows you to reach out and grow. If you are open to me and listen to me I will not fail you.

I am the messenger of rebirth:
Sometimes it is difficult to see how things can begin again. And yet you are born again every day, every day you have a new opportunity to start afresh. I represent the eternal return of the sun. Even for those in the darkness of depression, I bear the message of constantly renewed light.

I am the bird of love:
It is St. Paul who can speak best for me in Corinthians Chapter thirteen. He uses the word charity for love:

Though I speak with the tongues of men and of angels, and have not charity, I am become as sounding brass, or a tinkling cymbal.

And though I have the gift of prophecy, and understand all mysteries, and all knowledge; and though I have all faith, so that I could remove mountains, and have not charity, I am nothing.

And though I bestow all my goods to feed the poor, and though I give my body to be burned, and have not charity, it profiteth me nothing.

Charity suffereth long, and is kind; charity envieth not; charity vaunteth not itself, is not puffed up, Doth not behave itself unseemly, seeketh not her own, is not easily provoked, thinketh no evil;

Rejoiceth not in iniquity, but rejoiceth in the truth;

Beareth all things, believeth all things, hopeth all things, endureth all things.

Charity never faileth: but whether there be prophecies, they shall fail; whether there be tongues, they shall cease; whether there be knowledge, it shall vanish away.

For we know in part, and we prophesy in part.

But when that which is perfect is come, then that which is in part shall be done away. When I was a child, I spake as a child, I understood as a child, I thought as a child: but when I became a man, I put away childish things.

For now we see through a glass, darkly; but then face-to-face: now I know in part; but then shall I know even as also I am known.

And now abideth faith, hope and charity, these three, but the greatest of these is charity and the greatest of these is charity.

THE FALL OF A LEAF

Doves sweep upward, fluttering wing to wing,
Then turn, sun-caught, transparent tails on fire.
Higher they fly as if they are one wing
Swooping across the lovers' glass who tire
Of human love - its infidelities

And petty acts and watch the great white wing,
Lit by the morning light, dip down and rise,
Then break into a hundred doves who cling

Sharp-toed to umber tiles and hop and file
Domestically on the homely roof,
Separate and fussy. Then the lovers smile
Knowing there is sky vision and earth truth

And one reflects the other: love that soars
Makes rumpled beds and sweeps up dusty floors.

'James, James!' screamed Sophie. 'I've had enough, see, I've had enough. All you do is go out and booze and leave me here with the kids and no money. Well I'm telling you now, I'm not going on like this, not a moment longer. I'm off and you can bloody well look after them.'

James shouted back. 'One little drink after a hard days work, is that what you're objecting to?'

'It's not one, its every night. And you never ask me to go with you.'

'Some-one has to be with the kids.'

'Yes, well, it can be you now.'

She picked up her handbag and swung it in his face. 'At least my dad looks after me.'

Her father had come in earlier, found her weeping and given her some money. 'Well, you would go ahead,' he had said, patting her head. 'I told you then dear, without money love's an empty shell.'

Sophie walked out of the room, out of the door of their rented flat, and down the road towards the bus stop. She couldn't see for crying so she changed her mind and wandered onto the common that flanked the road. There was hardly anyone about, just the odd dog walker.

It was autumn and from somewhere there was a pungent smell of bonfire smoke that reminded her of her childhood when Dad had made bonfires in the garden. She would stand a little way off, fascinated by the golden curling flames. Things were different now. We have no house and no garden, she thought bitterly, and anyway bonfires aren't allowed.

A light November wind stirred and from the trees that lined the path leaves curled slowly and erratically down. If I could catch one I could have a wish, she said to herself, reliving her childhood again. As she spoke a leaf danced towards her and she bent forward and caught it. She cupped her other hand over it as if it was something precious. What shall I wish? To start again? But that's not possible. Besides, do I really want to? How can I even think of it? He goes to the pub because he hates his job. His boss bullies him but he can't leave because we need the money. So he drinks and I shout.

I wish for a way out, she whispered. She put the leaf into her pocket and wandered on until the path opened onto a wide stretch of grass. Then she heard the whirring of wings and several doves rose up above the trees from one of the houses that flanked the common. They swung into the wind together, like a great white wing then curved out of sight. Sophie held her breath. Birds of love.

My children, how could I walk out on my children? And James, how can I mind him having a drink after a work? He's always back for supper and sometimes he does the cooking and puts the children to bed.

I shout because I need a change.

But this **is** a change, she thought, I could walk here every evening after he comes in. It's a sort of freedom.

I have a husband, baby twins and my health. What am I thinking of? We must sort it out together, talk and not shout. We have too much to lose.

She walked slowly back to the house. The light was on in the bathroom. James was bathing the twins. They would be laughing and gurgling and splashing water over each other. She sat in the rickety chair the landlady had provided and listened. Then there was a ring at the bell. James hurried along the corridor, opened the door, welcomed someone and took her along to the bathroom. Sophie went cold with anger. Then James came into the living room and told Sophie Em from upstairs was going to baby sit and he was going to take her out. In future that's what they would do. Go out once a week together, as they used to. If he didn't go up the pub he could afford it. And he was going to look for another job. He wasn't going to put up with bullying any longer. Then he reassured her. 'I won't leave until I've found something else.'

Sophie wanted to run into his arms but instead she felt inside her pocket. 'Present,' she said, handing him the leaf.

It was a better present than money, she thought. Money was an empty shell without love.

8

The Cockerel

The cockerel that crows at dawn symbolizes the return of light and the resurrection of the spirit. It is a universal solar symbol, courageous, vigilant and in touch with the angels.

NORTH
On the topmost branch of Yggdrasil,
- The cosmic Ash appointed as look-out
By gods who fear the giants- the cockerel
Keeps an open eye through day and night.

EAST
In the courtyard of the Shinto temple
The ground is swept, blossom is alive
With scent, the sacred cockerel struts and calls
The goddess of the sun to leave her cave.

SOUTH
In Africa, the cock, depending on
Disguise, holds secrets, sometimes of betrayal.
The white Islamic cock, alert at dawn,
Crows to announce the presence of an angel.

WEST
The Western weathercock stands high; he roosts
On towers, swings on wind and nests in snow
And sun. He guards us from night's evil ghosts,
Proclaims the resurrection of the day.

THE SYMBOL OF THE COCKEREL IN MYTHOLOGY AND HISTORY

In **Judaism** the cockerel is associated with fertility. He and his hen are a symbol of the bride and groom at weddings. In the Talmud (the book of Jewish Civil and Canon law, written down by Judah 120 years after the destruction of the temple) the cock is a master of courtesy because he announces his Lord the Sun with a fanfare of crowing.

In **China** the white cockerel similarly protects the innocent against evil. The red cockerel keeps fire away. The cockerel is considered a beneficent bird because the Chinese ideogram for cock (KI) also means 'favourable' or a 'good omen'. The cockerel's appearance and behaviour also turns it into a suitable symbol of the 'five virtues' of the civil virtues. Its comb makes it resemble a mandarin or counsellor; it is a symbol of martial virtues because of its spurs and its courage in battle. It also symbolizes kindness because it shares its food with its hens and confidence because it announces dawn with constant accuracy.

In **Vietnam** a boiled cock's claw is used in fortune telling as it is seen as a symbol of the microcosm.

In **Japan** in the ancient Shinto belief, the cockerel's dawn crowing is a call to prayer. Its crowing is also linked to the songs of gods and each dawn it summons Amaterasu, Goddess of the Sun, from her cave. Beautiful cocks live in the grounds of the best known Shinto Temples where they are often depicted as part of the religious imagery of the temple. Sacred cocks are reared at the Ise Jingu temples.

In Ancient Greece a cock stood beside Leto as she gave birth to Artemis and Apollo. Their father was Zeus which made the cock sacred both to solar gods (Zeus and Apollo) and to lunar goddesses (Leto and Artemis). For this reason Pythagoras, the famous Greek mathematician, said cocks dedicated to Sun and Moon, should be cared for and not sacrificed. Nonetheless the cockerel was sacrificed to Aesculapius, the god of healing, and as such became a herald and messenger, guiding souls to the Otherworld, where they would wake to a new day.

In Nordic myths the cock symbolizes the attentive soldier who looks out from the top of the sacred ash for any giants who are preparing to fight the gods.

In Africa, to the Fulani (a mixed Mediterranean and Negro people scattered throughout Sudan eastward from Senegal) the cock represents secrets that differ according to his metamorphosed appearance and to where he is. For example a cock disguised as a ram in a yard is symbolic of the sort of secret told to relatives and close friends. A cock disguised as a bull in the street represents a secret told to everyone.

The Sudanese people of Mali think of the Cock's foot as a symbol of crossroads.

In Islam the cock is worshipped as the great bird Mahommed heard in the first heaven, crowing: There is no god but Allah.

In Christianity the cock is a sun symbol of Christ's light and resurrection. Weathercocks on the top of church spires are watchful guards against evil. Set on the highest point of holy buildings they symbolizes the supremacy of the spiritual. Because Christ said Peter would deny him three times before the cock crowed, the cock is a reminder of human weakness.

BIBLICAL QUOTATIONS

Matthew 26:34 Jesus said unto him, Verily I say unto thee, That this night, before the cock crow, thou shalt deny me thrice.

Mark 14:30 And Jesus saith unto him, Verily I say unto thee, That this day, even in this night, before the cock crow twice, though shalt deny me thrice.

Luke 22:34 And he said, I tell thee, Peter, the cock shall not crow this day, before that thou shalt thrice deny that thou knowest me.

Mark 13:35 Watch ye therefore: for ye know not when the master of the house cometh, at even, or at midnight, or at the cockcrowing, or in the morning.

COMMENT

Across the western world thousands of man-made cockerels stand guard on the spires of churches and the rooftops of temples. The cockerel symbolizes security and the return of light and as such speaks deeply to us. For surely our human happiness is a balance between a sense of renewal and a feeling of safety? When things go wrong it is often because we have lost one or the other. If our partner unexpectedly leaves us, the security of our belief in love and truth, which underlies any deep relationship, is swept away. When we are ill, played out or exhausted we long for a secure place in which we can slowly recover. Then as we get better, a feeling of renewed energy takes hold of us and we are literally born again. If society is disrupted by war security and renewal seem lost forever. Yet even under the most terrifying conditions the slow and constant rhythms of nature are there to help us. Night comes to renew our breadth of vision. By looking at stars in a clear sky we lose the straightjacket of time that binds our world. And yet because the moon never stops waxing and waning and the North star is always constant our sense of security is satisfied. Then day comes when there is chaos all around. But if we focus on, say, the petals of a single flower we will find them as refreshing as a night full of stars, and realize that, like stars, they respond to their own rhythm. So even in troubled times Nature provides us with her own beauty, her own stability and her own renewal.

WHAT DOES THE SYMBOL OF THE COCKEREL SAY TO US?

I am the herald of the dawn:
I am there in moments of depression and doubt to call you back to the creativity and warmth of a new day. I am forever vigilant and never fail to be there, calling you back, however dark and difficult things are.

I am always on guard against evil:
In today's world it is not always easy to see what is evil and what is not or indeed what we mean by evil. I am always watchful of evil and by contemplating my vigilance and my watchfulness, you will find it easier to understand how to be and how to act.

I am a symbol of God-given intelligence:
All our gifts are given to us by some grace we do not understand. We come by them and it is for us to make the most of them.

I escort the dead:
When we lose someone we love we always hope that they are led to the peace of eternal sleep or the peace of joyful enlightenment. To contemplate the great mystery of death in this way eases our grief a little by placing it in a context wider than the human heart.

RENEWAL

Along the dim horizon dawn lights hover
Delicate as butterflies; night yields
And at the edge of dark songbirds gather
Over milky barns and bristling fields.

Dreams have gone to nothing, light is pearl,
Towers absorb the sunrise, spires glow.
And now as if to keep a pact to call
And wake up half the world, the cockerel crows.

It was nearly dawn as Maggie tossed and turned, her thoughts and feelings like a swarm of wasps. At last she pushed back the duvet and crept in bare feet out of the bedroom, past the child's room and downstairs. She made herself a mug of hot chocolate then quietly unlocked the back door and went out into the small garden. It was the hour before the birds begin to sing. Herbs scented the air and behind the magnolia tree a new moon hung like a silver leaf. He has gone, she thought, pulling her fingers through her long black hair. This is the anniversary of his going and nothing has changed. I am left alone forever. The year has passed so slowly it feels more like ten years. I will never get over this.

Her pale delicate face reflected her thoughts. He had made his announcement suddenly, exactly a year ago, at about eight o'clock, when their daughter Emma was in bed and they were sitting in silence because there was nothing on the telly. There was no gentle preparation, no kindness, it was more like the sort of announcement you get on a railway station:.

Do not stand too near the edge of the platform. The next fast train will not be stopping.

He and his secretary were going to emigrate to Australia. He would make sure she was provided for. No, there was nothing to be done. He had made up his mind months ago. It was going to happen.

So this was why he had been silent for so long. She saw the tears in his eyes and knew that he was covering up his anguish at leaving Emma with a formality he used in his business life. But his manner made things worse, impossible to respond to, impossible to show anger. Maggie had nothing to say. She stood there helpless then turned and went into the kitchen. Later when she was alone in the house with her little daughter, she found four packets of aspirin and looked at them for a whole hour. Then she thought again. This was the time her daughter needed her more than anybody in the world.

The courtyard was peaceful but Maggie's thoughts were still inward. Why had Jay gone? Had her lack of trust initiated his affair? But how could she trust him when he was away half the time, 'on business' and she was excluded, always excluded.

She looked round. In a funny way she felt less lonely now. Here, in her little garden, she was at the centre of her own things. During the desolate months, while Emma was at nursery, she had tended her plants with intense care, anxious to keep every bush flourishing, every flower blooming, every herb growing. It was as if their beauty was vital to her existence. Looking after them had saved her from despair. The herbs were her favourites and she knew a lot about them. She breathed in their scent slowly, trying to still her heart's confusion. Then she followed the slow passage of the new moon through the magnolia tree like a meditation. After a long while she looked down at the herbs again, rosemary, thyme, mint, chive, vervain, marjoram, feverfew. Their presence soothed her, as if, without any interference, they were giving away their healing. As she looked at them, out of the blue, she remembered a poem about a herb speaking that she had learned at her convent school. It was by a German Abbess called Hildegard of Bingen who lived in the twelfth century and whose knowledge of herbs and their medicinal uses was second to none. Maggie wondered how something written in the twelfth century could be so meaningful in the twenty-first. Or was it that nothing really changed?

I am a soothing herb. I dwell in dew
And air and in all greenness and my heart
Is filled to overflowing., I help others.

I was there when the first words resounded:
'Let there be.' I know the needs of life
I lift the broken hearted, lead them on
To wholeness. I am balm for every pain.

She kept repeating the poem under her breath and after a while, without any effort, she felt the first shoots of hope grow in her heart, replacing the whirl of emotions that had kept her awake. *There is a future for me, there is a place for me.* Tears of relief welled up in her eyes and when she heard the cock crow she smiled with a sense of renewal. She went back to bed and fell into a deep dreamless sleep. Later she woke to Emma leaning over her, running her fingers down her cheeks. Maggie sat up and hugged her daughter. 'I have a big new idea Emma and you are the first to hear it. Next year when you go to school I will go as well. Only at my school I will learn to be a herbalist. That's what I'm going to be. For the first time, Emma, for the first time for ages and ages and ages I can see a path into the future.'

9

The Dragon

The dragon is a fabulous and universal creature that has many differing shapes and symbolic meaning, many of them good. But in the West, since Medieval times, the dragon has mainly symbolized the devil, the primordial enemy that must be overcome.

I am fabulous, many faced.
In the East, rain dragon,
White beast of the moon,

Graced with sharp sight. Painted red
I dance on flags, yet I am
Thief, malevolent guardian

Of the West. Myth-bred Apollo
Fought me,
St Michael the Archangel slew me,

And in the glowing twilight
Between myth and truth
St George pierced me. In the forge

Of his faith, the flames of his courage,
He hammered a bright coin, a new sun,
To shine again over the frozen kingdom.

THE SYMBOL OF THE DRAGON IN MYTHOLOGY AND HISTORY

The dragon seems to be an amalgam of elements taken from various animals that are especially dangerous and aggressive like crocodiles, serpents, pre-historic animals and lions.

In Egypt the dragon was an emblem of Osiris, the Egyptian god of the underworld. It was believed the dragon caused the annual flooding of the Nile, thus bringing fertility to the earth.

In China dragons were part of the landscape. For instance, a chain of hills was seen as the spine of a dragon. The energy of local dragons was always considered when a new building was to be erected. Chinese dragons are aquatic, aerial and subterranean, and epitomize imperial power. In esoteric Chinese thought, the red dragon is a symbol for science, the white dragon a symbol of the moon and in ancient Chinese writings the dragon is often associated with rain, lightning and fecundity. The Chinese dragon also symbolizes strength and speed and is the intermediary between the highest spirituality and ordinary physical life. The conquered dragon is a symbol of victory over evil and the hidden forces beneath the earth.

In Greece a dragon embodied the energies that came out of a rock crevice at Delphi.

The Dragon is a symbol of plagues and sickness and is sometimes related to ogres. It is also a symbol of the Guardian, for it is strong and vigilant with sharp eyesight.

The Gnostic dragon, depicted biting its own tail, is a symbol of time and the rhythmic cycles of life, the way through all things.

In the Middle Ages dragons are shown with the head of an eagle, the body of a huge serpent, the wings of a bat and a forked tail twisting back on itself. The eagle represents its celestial powers, the serpent its secret hidden self, the wings its intellect and the tail its submission to reason.

In alchemy the dragon is the symbol of burning thirst and hunger, the blind impulses towards self-gratification, while fighting dragons symbolize psychic disintegration.

In esoteric Hebraic tradition perhaps the most intriguing interpretation of dragons is found. It insists that the meaning of the dragon must remain inviolate.

BIBLICAL QUOTATIONS

Ezekiel 29:3 Speak and say, Thus sayeth the Lord God; Behold, I am against thee, Pharaoh king of Egypt, the great dragon that lieth in the midst of his rivers, which hath said, My river is mine own, and I have made it for myself.

Micah 1:8 Therefore I will wail and howl, I will go stripped and naked: I will make a wailing like the dragons, and mourning as the owls.

Job 30:29 I am a brother to dragons, and a companion to owls.

Revelation 12:3-4 And there appeared another wonder in heaven; and behold a great red dragon, having seven heads and ten horns, and seven crowns upon his heads. And his tail drew the third part of the stars of heaven, and did cast them to the earth: and the dragon stood before the woman which was ready to be delivered, for to devour her child as soon as it was born.

Revelation 12:7-9 And there was war in heaven: Michael and his angels fought against the dragon; and the dragon fought and his angels, And prevailed not; neither was their place found any more in heaven. And the great dragon was cast out, that old serpent, called the Devil, and Satan, which deceiveth the whole world: he was cast out into the earth, and his angels were cast out with him.

Isaiah 34:13 And thorns shall come up in her palaces, nettles and brambles in the fortresses thereof: and it shall be an habitation of dragons, and a court for owls.

Isaiah 43:20 The beast of the field shall honour me, the dragons and the owls: because I give waters in the wilderness, and rivers in the desert, to give drink to my people, my chosen.

COMMENTARY

In the West the dragon is the symbol of the evil enemy, fought and conquered by many heroes. As such the dragon helps us to come face to face with what we must fight in our own lives. For we all have enemies, real and imaginary, without and within, and we must overcome them to find the treasure of life again, as St. George fought his dragon and released the princess.

This evil enemy has many disguises: Pride, Wrath, Envy, Lust, Gluttony, Avarice, Sloth - the seven deadly sins cover most things. It is by facing evil in whatever form it has taken, and by acknowledging it, that we take the first steps towards enlightenment. For it is only when we face, recognize and understand our human fallibility that we are able to forgive others and ourselves: *For if ye forgive men their trespasses your heavenly Father will also forgive you. Matthew 6:14*

To take one example out of many that we read about and see around us: In our modern world children are faced with a widespread drug culture. Very many young people have to fight this particular dragon.

WHAT DOES THE SYMBOL OF THE DRAGON SAY TO US?

I teach you to come face to face with evil:
In Christian art I symbolize Satan or sin: when I lie at the feet of the Virgin Mary or Christ I represent conquered evil. In the

pictures of St. Michael and St. Margaret I typify their conquest over Satan. Many saints have come face to face with me and by slaughtering me have shown the victory of good over evil: It is the same for you. It is only by coming face to face with evil and acknowledging it, that you can conquer it.

I guard the treasure of your life:
As St. George fought me to rescue the princess, you too can fight me to free your heart and retrieve the treasure of love.

I am the bringer of rain:
By acknowledging me you may bring refreshment to a parched land.

I am a source of heroism:
Because I represent something terrible to overcome, I am your means of becoming a hero or a heroine. For those who fight evil, though they may not be acknowledged, are people of very great courage and hope.

NO

'Snow!'* ordered the dragon.
The girl shivered, cowered
Before its claws, its eagle head.
The dragon, empowered
With snow magic, uttered a pagan
Spell. Then sack cloths,

Winding sheets of snow
Fell on her, pelted her.
She was a bird in a storm
Snow struck, unsheltered,
Until a song of long ago
Sang on her breath.

Caught in its own spell
The dragon left in a tumult
Of snow and the girl rose,
Free of its assault,
Gently singing the carol's
Forgotten truth.
*Snow is slang for cocaine or heroin.

She was not alone in the Rehabilitation Centre, yet she had never been more lonely in her life. It was December. She was sixteen and locked up. No that wasn't true. The door was there, she could walk out if she wanted to. She could pack her small suit case and go.

'You have three chances,' they told her. 'If you go three times you won't be allowed to get back.'

The drug rehabilitation Centre was sparsely furnished but brightly painted. She had a room to herself and nobody minded what she did as long as she didn't smoke or inject. They were the only other rules.

The plain brick building was surrounded by a wild garden where you took your visitors. For the first month you had to stick it out alone. After that they could come once a week.

They!

I mean Mum and Dad

Mum, I never thought it would come to this. Dad I never wanted..

Or did she?

She lay flat on her back, wondering what Gus was doing. Gustave: French, pale,in love with heroin. It was he who had led her through the gateway to heaven and hell. He was waiting for her. At a moment's notice he would take her by the hand and lead her once more through the gate.

She reached for her mobile. He had already sent her a pleading message. She began to press the buttons. His numbers stood out on the screen like a password to her old life. One press of the button and she would hear his compelling French accent. Her old life was a voice away.

Instead - and she never quite knew what impelled her to do it -she flung the mobile at the wall and watched it crash down onto the wooden boards.

'Tea's ready.' said Lunna at the door. 'Come on. Afterwards we're going to make pots.'

Wearily she slid off the bed and followed Lunna into the kitchen.

The mugs were red, yellow, blue, green. Cheer up said the mugs. The tea gave her a big hug. It was just as well for the others were older than she was and said very little to each other, too absorbed in their own pain to pay much attention to each other.

In the art therapy room she felt like a seven year old. She remembered once making little things for her doll's house, poking and pushing the plasticine until shapes formed under her fingers.

'Making is our salvation,' her art teacher had once said and they had all giggled. Now as her fingers dipped and kneaded and shaped the lump of wet clay she had scraped from the bucket, she felt something buzz and stir inside her. Was this salvation? Without too much thought she made a child sitting on the floor, knees up, thin arms holding a book. It was the book Dad had read to her the year before he had moved out.

'That's great,' said Lunna, but she didn't reply. She didn't want to share her creation. For once it mattered to her. Strangely and miraculously it had given her a long forgotten sense of freedom. Maybe her teacher had been right She took her model into her bedroom and placed it on the radiator to dry. She flung herself on the bed.

Ten minutes later her mobile rang again. She looked at it for a long time then switched it off.

Sources

Holy Bible: King James' Version Teachers' Edition, Collins

Lady of the Beasts :The Goddess and her Sacred Animals, Buffie Johnson Inner Traditions 1987

The Golden Bough: A study in Magic and Religion.

J. G. Frazer, The Macmillan Press 1976

Helps to the Study of the Bible Oxford University Press, Larousse Encyclopaedia of Mythology, Paul Hamlyn 1965

Greek Myths, Robert Graves, Penguin 1985

A Dictionary of Symbols, J.E.Curlot, translated from the Spanish by Jacki Sage, Routledge and Kegan Paul 1981

The Hutchinson Encyclopedia of Living Faiths, edited by R.C. Zaehner, Helicon 2001

The Masks of God: Primitive Mythology, Oriental Mythology, Occidental Mythology, Joseph Campbell Souvenir Press 2001

Buddhist Scriptures, Penguin Classics

The Bhagavad Gita, Penguin Classics

The Language of Symbols, David Fontana, Duncan Baird Publishers

The Penguin Dictionary of Symbols, Jean Chevalir and Alain Gheerbrant, translated from the French by John Buchanan-Brown Penguin 1996

Oriental Mythology, Joseph Campbell, Souvenir Press 2000

Circle Books

Circle is a symbol of infinity and unity. It's part of a growing list of imprints, including o-books.net and zero-books.net.

Circle Books aims to publish books in Christian spirituality that are fresh, accessible, and stimulating.

Our books are available in all good English language bookstores worldwide. If you can't find the book on the shelves, then ask your bookstore to order it for you, quoting the ISBN and title. Or, you can order online—all major online retail sites carry our titles.

To see our list of titles, please view www.Circle-Books.com, growing by 80 titles per year.

Authors can learn more about our proposal process by going to our website and clicking on Your Company > Submissions.

We define Christian spirituality as the relationship between the self and its sense of the transcendent or sacred, which issues in literary and artistic expression, community, social activism, and practices. A wide range of disciplines within the field of religious studies can be called upon, including history, narrative studies, philosophy, theology, sociology, and psychology. Interfaith in approach, Circle Books fosters creative dialogue with non-Christian traditions.

And tune into MySpiritRadio.com for our book review radio show, hosted by June-Elleni Laine, where you can listen to authors discussing their books.

mySpiritRadio